History Alive!®
The Ancient World

Ignite students' passion for history and bring learning alive in your classroom today! Using the highly acclaimed TCI Approach, teach a complete TCI lesson with the materials in this booklet.

See page 15.

TCi®
Teachers' Curriculum Institute

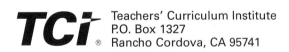 Teachers' Curriculum Institute
P.O. Box 1327
Rancho Cordova, CA 95741

Customer Service: 800-497-6138
www.teachtci.com

ISBN 1-58371-366-2
1 2 3 4 5 6 7 8 9 10   09 08 07 06 05

TCI Brings Learning Alive!

History Alive! The Ancient World is part of the TCI core program family and is available for use in your classroom today. We believe that this complete sample lesson—though just a snapshot of the program—will help you experience the TCI Approach in an exciting and engaging way.

This comprehensive program, with all the essential components to achieve a student-centered classroom, does the following:

- Uses multiple intelligence teaching strategies that engage all learners.
- Connects learning to students' prior knowledge and experience.
- Challenges students to process new knowledge through higher-order thinking skills.
- Supports reading in the social studies classroom through considerate text.
- Focuses on critical thinking and understanding.
- Helps you create a cooperative, tolerant classroom where students take responsibility for their own behavior.
- Improves students' test scores while increasing their content literacy.

All the core materials that you need to teach the featured sample lesson are included in this booklet. These include resources for teachers (the Lesson Guide, with the Guide to Reading Notes and assessment masters) and for students (the Interactive Student Notebook, the Student Edition, and other reproducible materials).

TCI is committed to bringing learning alive for all learners. If you have any questions about how to use these materials in your classroom or implement the program at your school, please call TCI Customer Support at 800-497-6138.

Founders
Bert Bower   Jim Lobdell

Bert Bower

Jim Lobdell

Enhance your students' learning with the teaching practices of the highly acclaimed TCI Approach. *History Alive! The Ancient World* combines hands-on activities with a readable Student Edition to provide you with a comprehensive and effective way to teach ancient world history.

Teacher Resources
Item No. 350-6sam

This full-year program includes all the materials you need for engaging instruction.
- Lesson Guides include thoughtfully prepared, step-by-step procedures for each activity.
- Student Edition includes comprehensive content, easy-to-read text, and dynamic photos that add depth to the material.
- Interactive Student Notebook triggers content memory.
- Full-color Transparencies and Placards allow for students' visual discovery.
- Sounds of History CD provides dramatic recordings and musical selections to fully engage students in activities.
- Digital Teacher Resources CD-ROM contains an Assessment Bank and digital versions of the Lesson Guides, Interactive Student Notebook, transparencies, and audio materials. These digital versions allow you to customize assessments and transparencies for individual classroom and student needs.

Special Features
- Geography Challenge lessons at the beginning of each unit allow students to apply their geography skills.
- Timeline Challenge lessons at the end of each unit provide students with a comprehensive visual reference for time and place throughout their study of the ancient world.
- Online Resources help students extend learning beyond the lessons, with additional resources that include biographies, literature, primary sources, Internet projects and links, and enrichment essays related to ancient world history.

Student Edition
Item No. 351-4sam

This Student Edition is a colorful, considerate text that builds content literacy. Along with each Student Edition you will also receive gratis one Interactive Student Notebook.

Interactive Student Notebook
Item No. 370-0sam (package of 5)

You may order additional copies of *History Alive! The Ancient World* Interactive Student Notebook as needed in packages of 5.

For more information and current pricing, contact Customer Service or visit TCI on the web today!

Phone: 800-497-6138
Fax: 800-343-6828
Web: www.teachtci.com
Email: info@teachtci.com

What's in This Sample Lesson Booklet

Note: For this sample lesson booklet, the full-color Student Edition, Transparencies, and Placards have been rendered as black-and-white masters so that you can easily copy them for classroom use. If you have any of these components in their original color format, you need not copy the masters provided here.

The TCI Approach

The TCI Approach consists of a series of instructional practices that allow students of all abilities to experience key social studies concepts.

THEORY-BASED ACTIVE INSTRUCTION

STANDARDS-BASED CONTENT

Dynamic lessons build mastery of state and national social studies standards. Integrates hands-on active learning, achieving a consistent pattern of high-quality social studies instruction while being mindful of standards.

PREVIEW ASSIGNMENT

A short, engaging assignment at the start of each lesson helps you preview key concepts and tap students' prior knowledge and personal experience.

MULTIPLE INTELLIGENCE TEACHING STRATEGIES

CONSIDERATE TEXT

Carefully structured reading materials enable students at all levels to understand what they read. Recognizes that a successful reading of expository text involves four stages: previewing the content, reading, taking notes, and processing the content, or reviewing and applying what has been learned.

GRAPHICALLY ORGANIZED READING NOTES

Comprehensive graphic organizers, used to record key ideas, further help students obtain meaning from what they read. Graphic organizers help students see the underlying logic and interconnections among concepts by improving their comprehension and retention in the subject area.

PROCESSING ASSIGNMENT

An end-of-lesson Processing assignment, involving multiple intelligences and higher-order thinking skills, challenges students to apply what they learned. It helps students to synthesize and apply the information they have learned in a variety of creative ways.

MULTIPLE INTELLIGENCE ASSESSMENT

Carefully designed tests encourage students to use their various intelligences to demonstrate their understanding of key concepts while preparing them for standardized tests.

Lessons and activities are based on three well-established theories:

THEORY-BASED ACTIVE INSTRUCTION

Multiple Intelligences According to Howard Gardner's revolutionary theory, every student is intelligent—just not in the same way. Because everyone learns in a different way, the best activities tap more than one kind of intelligence. Gardner has described these seven intelligences: verbal-linguistic, logical-mathematical, visual-spatial, body-kinesthetic, musical-rhythmic, interpersonal, and intrapersonal.

Cooperative Interaction Elizabeth Cohen's research has led her to conclude that cooperative groupwork leads to learning gains and to higher student achievement. Cohen has found that if students are trained in cooperative behaviors, placed in mixed-ability groups, and assigned roles to complete during a multiple-ability task, they tend to interact more equally. This increased student interaction leads to more learning and greater content retention.

Spiral Curriculum Educational theorist Jerome Bruner championed the idea of the spiral curriculum, in which students learn progressively more difficult concepts through a process of step-by-step discovery. With this approach, all students can learn once a teacher has shown them how to think and discover knowledge for themselves.

Multiple Intelligence Teaching Strategies incorporate six types of activities:

MULTIPLE INTELLIGENCE TEACHING STRATEGIES

Visual Discovery
Students view, touch, interpret, and bring to life compelling images, turning what is usually a passive, teacher-centered activity—lecturing—into a dynamic, participative experience.

Social Studies Skill Builder
This strategy turns the traditional, rote tasks usually associated with skill-based worksheets into more dynamic, interactive activities.

Experiential Exercise
These short, memorable activities make abstract ideas or remote events accessible and meaningful by tapping into intrapersonal and body-kinesthetic intelligences.

Writing for Understanding
Writing for Understanding activities give all learners, even those with lesser linguistic skills, something memorable to write about.

Response Groups
This strategy helps students grapple with the ambiguities of issues in social studies, recognize the complexity of historical events, and discuss the consequences of public policies.

Problem Solving Groupwork
This strategy teaches students the skills necessary to work together successfully in small groups, both in the classroom and later in life.

Program Contents

UNIT 1

Early Humans and the Rise of Civilization

Ancient Egypt and the Near East

Program Contents

UNIT 3

Ancient India

Ancient China

Program Contents

UNIT 5

Ancient Greece

Ancient Rome

Program Components

Lesson Guide

- Taps students' multiple intelligences with interactive classroom activities
- Provides simple step-by-step procedures for each activity
- Contains reproducible student and teacher materials
- Lists required materials
- Includes easy-to-use assessment tools

Student Edition

- Integrates reading with multiple intelligence activities in the classroom
- Offers well-structured and manageable chapters to help all students succeed
- Defines key vocabulary in margins
- Provides graphic organizers at the beginning of each chapter for students' use throughout the lesson
- Enhances text with meaningful historical images
- Provides considerate text for students at all levels

Interactive Student Notebook

- Engages student interest with Preview pages
- Enhances student understanding through Reading and Activity Notes
- Helps students master new concepts and skills with Processing assignments

Transparency Book

- Provides vibrant color transparencies
- Builds and enhances visual literacy skills
- Offers a meaningful glimpse into other times and other places

Placard Set

- Provides dozens of full-color laminated picture cards
- Corresponds to hands-on activities
- Taps students' visual skills during active learning sessions

Sounds of History CD

- Stimulates learning with musical recordings, dramatic readings, and audio effects
- Enhances the drama and realism of many student activities

Digital Teacher Resources CD-ROM

- Contains an Assessment Bank and digital versions of the Lesson Guides, Interactive Student Notebook, transparencies, and Sounds of History audio materials
- Enables teachers to customize assessments and transparencies

How to Teach This Lesson

Was Ancient Sumer a Civilization?

In this lesson, students first read about characteristics of a civilization in a **Social Studies Skill Builder**. They use their new knowledge to analyze artifacts from ancient Sumer to determine whether ancient Sumer was a civilization. Then, in a Processing assignment, they find contemporary artifacts to use as evidence of civilization today.

The following pages contain all the printed materials you need to teach this lesson from *History Alive! The Ancient World.* Follow these steps:

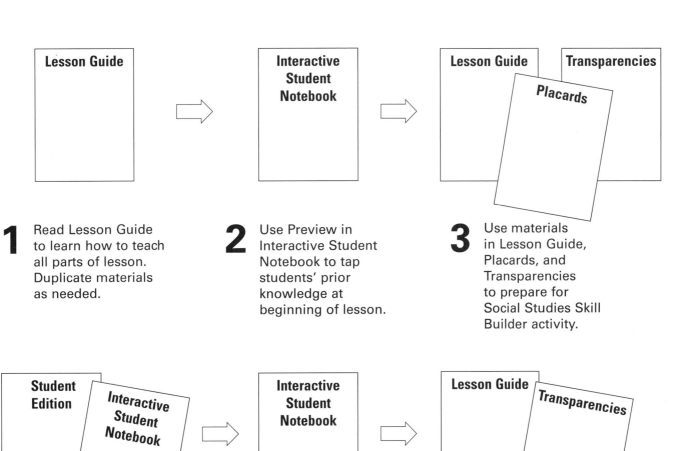

1 Read Lesson Guide to learn how to teach all parts of lesson. Duplicate materials as needed.

2 Use Preview in Interactive Student Notebook to tap students' prior knowledge at beginning of lesson.

3 Use materials in Lesson Guide, Placards, and Transparencies to prepare for Social Studies Skill Builder activity.

4 Have students read Student Edition during classroom activity and use Interactive Student Notebook to record reading notes.

5 Direct students to complete Processing assignment in Interactive Student Notebook to apply what they have learned.

6 Use assessment in Lesson Guide, with related Transparencies, to measure what students have learned.

Was Ancient Sumer a Civilization?

Overview

In this lesson, students first read about characteristics of civilization in a **Social Studies Skill Builder**. They use their new knowledge to analyze artifacts from ancient Sumer to determine whether ancient Sumer was a civilization. Then, in a Processing assignment, they find contemporary artifacts to use as evidence of civilization today.

Objectives

Students will

- identify characteristics of civilization.
- analyze artifacts from ancient Sumer and explain how they are examples of the various characteristics of civilization.
- identify modern-day artifacts that are examples of characteristics of civilization.

Materials

- *History Alive! The Ancient World*
- Interactive Student Notebooks
- Transparencies 5A and 5B
- Information Master 5A (several copies on card stock)
- Information Master 5B (1 transparency)
- Placards 5A–5H (2 sets)
- CD Track 6
- transparent tape

Note: This lesson uses the audio CD that is included with *History Alive! The Ancient World.* Track 6, a recording of string music from the Near East, adds an aural dimension to the image of an ancient lyre on Placard 5H, but the sample lesson can be completed without this music.

Preview

Have students turn to Preview 5 in their Interactive Student Notebooks. Review the directions with them, and answer any questions they have. After they have completed their diagrams describing characteristics of a "highly civilized" society, have them share their ideas with a partner, or have several volunteers briefly share their work with the class. Explain to students that in the following activity, they will investigate whether ancient Sumer had the characteristics of civilization.

Graphic Organizer

1 Have students read Section 5.1 of *History Alive! The Ancient World*. Have them identify what they will learn about in this chapter. Make sure they understand the meanings of the boldfaced key terms, which are defined in the Glossary. (**Note:** You may want to have students use the Prereading Handout on page xvii of this Lesson Guide to conduct a prereading of the chapter. [Not required for sample lesson. The Prereading Handout is one of the ways this program supports students in reading expository text.])

2 Introduce the graphic organizer. Have students examine the graphic organizer in Section 5.1. Ask, *What kind of diagram is this? What is the main topic of this spoke diagram? What characteristics of civilization are shown on this spoke diagram?*

Reading for Understanding

Have students read Section 5.2 in their books. When they are finished, ask, *What characteristics of civilization will we learn about in this chapter? What everyday objects might be examples of these characteristics? What kinds of things might ancient Sumerians have left behind that could be examples of these characteristics?*

Social Studies Skill Builder

1 Prepare your classroom for the activity. Follow these steps:

- Post the two sets of *Placards 5A–5G: Artifacts from Ancient Sumer* on the walls along opposite sides of the room.
- Post the two copies of *Placard 5H: Artifact from Ancient Sumer* together. Place the CD player near them, and cue the CD to Track 6, "Essence Arabe."
- Create several dice for the activity using *Information Master 5A: Die Template*. Place the dice in a central location.

2 Put students into mixed-ability pairs. You may want to create a class seating chart on a transparency to show students who their partners are and where to sit.

3 Explain the objective of the activity. Tell students that in this activity they will learn about characteristics of civilization. They will determine whether ancient Sumer had each characteristic by analyzing and drawing sound conclusions from artifacts that archeologists have unearthed.

4 Explain the activity. Have students open their Interactive Student Notebooks to Reading Notes 5. Project a transparency of *Information Master 5B: Steps for Analyzing Artifacts* and review the steps for completing the activity. Answer any questions students have. (**Note:** You may want to review the definition of *primary* and *secondary sources* by having students identify which type of source the artifacts represent, and which type of source the information in their text represents. You might also briefly discuss the credibility of these sources in learning about ancient Sumer.)

5 Practice the steps for analyzing an ancient Sumerian artifact as a class. Ask students to read Section 5.3, which is about ensuring a stable food supply, and have pairs complete the steps on Information Master 5B. Encourage them to find *as many artifacts as possible* that are examples of this characteristic of civilization. Then have volunteers share their ideas from their Reading Notes with the class.

6 Conduct the Social Studies Skill Builder. Project Information Master 5B during the activity as reference. Have pairs come to you to have their work checked for the first two sections of the Reading Notes they complete. If they are following directions accurately, consider circulating around the room to spot-check work rather than checking each pair's work for every section of the Reading Notes. Tell students to play CD Track 6 when they inspect Placard 5H.

7 Conduct a wrap-up activity. This wrap-up activity will allow students to share their ideas and emphasize that a single artifact can provide evidence for more than one characteristic of civilization. After most pairs have learned about most of the characteristics of civilization, follow these steps for the wrap-up activity "Last One Standing":

- Have each pair determine who will be their first "stander."
- Select one of the artifact placards at random and show it to the class.
- Have pairs check their Reading Notes to see if they used this artifact as evidence of *one or more* of the characteristics of civilization. If so, their stander should stand up.
- Ask a couple of standers to share their explanation of how this artifact is evidence for *one* characteristic of civilization.
- Next, ask the standers who used this artifact as evidence for *two or more* characteristics to remain standing while the others sit down. Ask a couple of them to share how this artifact is evidence for a different characteristic of civilization.

- Continue this process until one student is the "last one standing."
- Select a new placard and repeat the activity. (**Note:** It is sufficient to do this for only a few of the eight placards.)

Processing

Review the instructions for completing Processing 5 in the Interactive Student Notebook. Answer any questions students have. When students have finished their spoke diagrams, have them share some of their modern examples of characteristics of civilization in a class discussion.

Assessment

Masters for assessment appear on the next three pages. Project *Transparency 5A: The Standard of Ur* and *Transparency 5B: Overlay for Assessment 5* for students to view while they complete Item 10.

1. C   2. A   3. B   4. B   5. C
6. D   7. A   8. B

9. *inner circle:* ziggurat, government officials, priests, slaves (belonging to upper classes); *middle circle:* craftspeople, merchants; *outer circle:* farmers, farms, irrigation ditches
10. The bulleted points can provide a rubric for this item.

Online Resources

For more information on Unit 1: Early Humans and the Rise of Civilization, refer students to Online Resources for *History Alive! The Ancient World* at www.historyalive.com/historyalive, where they will find the following resources and assignments:
- excerpts from primary sources and literature
- a biography of an individual important to the study of early civilization
- links to related Web sites for more in-depth exploration
- an Internet research project
- enrichment essays

Options for Students with Special Needs

See pages 30–31 for tips on adapting this lesson to meet the needs of
- English language learners.
- learners reading and writing below grade level.
- learners with special education needs.
- advanced learners.

Fill in the bubble beside the best answer to each question.

1. Ancient Sumerians invented irrigation systems and plows. What did these two inventions help provide?
   Ⓐa system of government
   Ⓑa partner with whom to trade
   Ⓒa steady supply of food
   Ⓓan honor for the gods

2. What evidence shows that Sumerian society developed after the Stone Age?
   Ⓐcopper blades
   Ⓑpainted pottery
   Ⓒwooden plows
   Ⓓmud houses

3. What ancient Sumerian most likely spoke the words below?

   "I live in a two-story house near the center of the city. I like to throw parties where my guests eat from gold plates and drink from gold cups."

   Ⓐa farmer
   Ⓑa government official
   Ⓒa craftsperson
   Ⓓa merchant

4. Which statement shows how Sumerian religion and government were connected?
   ⒶSumerians believed that merchants sold goods for the king.
   ⒷSumerians believed that the king got power from the gods.
   ⒸSumerians recorded their prayers on clay tablets.
   ⒹSumerians recorded the movements of the planets.

5. The Sumerians invented something that made it possible for their armies to use chariots. What was it?
   Ⓐharnesses
   Ⓑswords
   Ⓒwheels
   Ⓓhorseshoes

6. What evidence shows that Sumerians were not prehistoric?
   Ⓐziggurats
   Ⓑstatues
   Ⓒirrigation ditches
   Ⓓwritten laws

7. Whose duty was it to do these jobs: build temples, lead the army, and enforce laws?
   Ⓐthe king's
   Ⓑthe priests'
   Ⓒthe scribes'
   Ⓓthe governors'

8. The artifact pictured below is evidence of what part of Sumerian civilization?
   Ⓐreligion
   Ⓑgovernment
   Ⓒthe arts
   Ⓓtechnology

Use your knowledge of social studies to complete the item below.

9. The circles below represent a Sumerian city. The inner circle is the center of the city. The two outer circles show more distant parts of the city. Put each item from the Word Bank on the part of the city where it belongs.

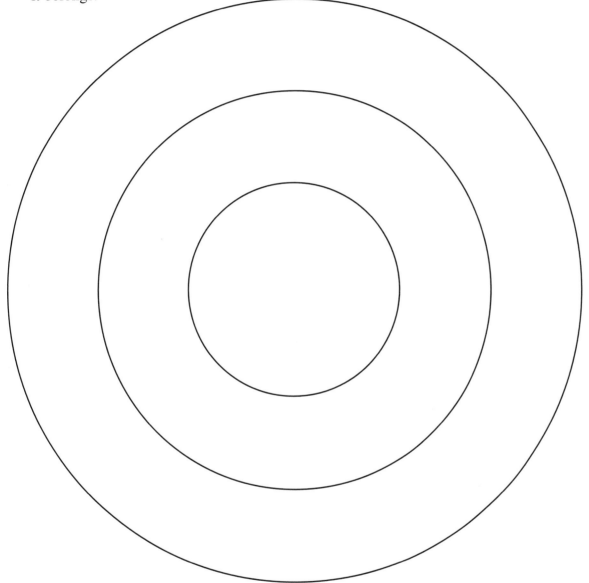

Word Bank		
craftspeople	government officials	priests
farmers	irrigation ditches	slaves
farms	merchants	ziggurat

Follow the directions to complete the item below.

10. The Standard of Ur is the most famous artifact ever recovered from ancient Sumer. Carefully examine the Standard of Ur on the transparency. Notice that some parts of it have been circled and numbered.

   • Select three numbered parts that you think represent different characteristics of civilization.

   • In each sentence below, identify one of the numbered parts you selected and complete the sentence.

Part _____ of the Standard of Ur represents _____

(characteristic of civilization)

because _____

_____

_____ .

Part _____ of the Standard of Ur represents _____

(characteristic of civilization)

because _____

_____

_____ .

Part _____ of the Standard of Ur represents _____

(characteristic of civilization)

because _____

_____

_____ .

Die Template

To create a die, copy this page onto card stock. Cut the template along the solid lines, fold it along the dashed lines, and tape it together to create a cube.

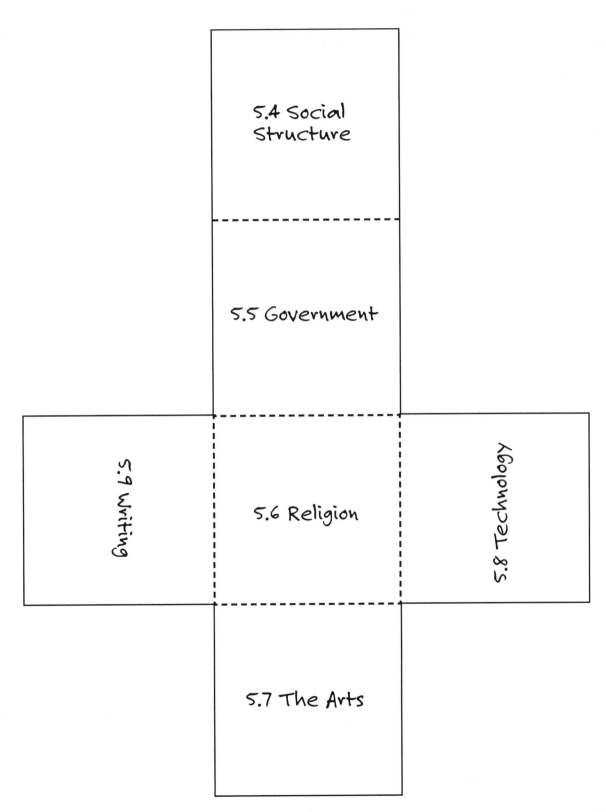

Follow these steps to analyze the artifacts from ancient Sumer:

1. Roll one of the dice to determine which characteristic of civilization you will read about. If you have already read this section, roll again.

2. Read the corresponding section in Chapter 5 of *History Alive! The Ancient World*.

3. Carefully examine the artifacts posted around the room and read the accompanying archeologist's notes. Find *as many artifacts as possible* that are examples of the characteristic of civilization you just read about.

4. Complete the corresponding section of your Reading Notes. *For each artifact you choose,* remember to make a simple sketch and to complete the sentence about how it relates to that characteristic of civilization.

5. Bring your Reading Notes to your teacher to be checked. Then start over at Step 1.

After reading one section of Chapter 5 in *History Alive! The Ancient World* and analyzing all the artifacts from ancient Sumer, follow these steps:

1. Find the oval in the diagrams on this and the following three pages that corresponds to the section you read.

2. In the space around that oval, make a simple drawing of *each artifact* you analyzed that you think is an example of that characteristic of civilization.

3. Next to each drawing, complete this sentence: *(Name of artifact) relates to this characteristic of civilization because…*

4. Complete the spoke diagram by connecting each drawing to the oval with a line.

Possible answers:

**5.3
Stable Food
Supply**

The clay tablet relates to this characteristic of civilization because it tells that the Sumerians raised barley.

The stone seal showing plowing relates to this characteristic of civilization because it shows Sumerians preparing fields.

The clay tablet relates to this characteristic of civilization because it indicates a class of scribes and workers.

The clay seal of the king appointing a governor relates to this characteristic of civilization because it shows a government class.

The statue of a chariot relates to this characteristic of civilization because it shows a military class.

The gold cup relates to this characteristic of civilization because it indicates a craftsperson and an upper class.

The lyre relates to this characteristic of civilization because it indicates a craftsperson and an upper class that is entertained by music.

5.4 Social Structure

Characteristics of Civilization

5.5 Government

The clay tablet relates to this characteristic of civilization because it shows that government officials distributed grain.

The clay seal relates to this characteristic of civilization because it indicates there were governors and a king.

The copper statue of a chariot relates to this characteristic of civilization because it shows there was an army.

The statue of a king carrying a basket relates to this characteristic of civilization because it illustrates there was a king.

The lyre relates to this characteristic of civilization because it indicates there was a queen.

Possible answers:

5.6 Religion

The statue of a married couple relates to this characteristic of civilization because it was found in a shrine and might have been a gift to the gods.

The statue of a king carrying a basket relates to this characteristic of civilization because it indicates that one of the king's duties was to build temples.

The stone seal relates to this characteristic of civilization because it shows two gods.

Characteristics of Civilization

5.7 The Arts

The statue of a married couple relates to this characteristic of civilization because it shows there were sculptors.

The gold cup relates to this characteristic of civilization because it shows there were skilled metalworkers.

The statue of a king carrying a basket relates to this characteristic of civilization because it shows they had metalworkers and architects for the temples.

The lyre relates to this characteristic of civilization because it shows Sumerians had music.

5.8 Technology

The copper statue of a chariot relates to this characteristic of civilization because it shows the Sumerians had developed the wheel.

5.9 Writing

The clay tablet relates to this characteristic of civilization because it has writing on it.

The stone seal relates to this characteristic of civilization because it has writing on it.

The statue of a king carrying a basket relates to this characteristic of civilization because it has writing on it.

The clay seal relates to this characteristic of civilization because it has writing on it.

Was Ancient Sumer a Civilization?

English Language Learners

Modify Processing 5 to require less written work. Ask that students find or draw pictures for each of the seven characteristics of civilization, but for the sentence-completion step, allow them to choose just three or four of the characteristics.

Learners Reading and Writing Below Grade Level

Encourage students to use colored pencils or pens to complete their Reading Notes. Suggest that they use a different color for each section of text covered by the spoke diagram. This can help students group their thoughts and will clarify the separation between the several sections.

Learners with Special Education Needs

Have students create a set of vocabulary cards before reading this chapter. On each card, students write the word and its definition and draw a picture to depict the meaning. Suggest that students include each of the seven characteristics of a civilization in this set of cards.

For Reading Notes 5, have students complete Steps 1, 2, and 4 independently. For Step 3, have them simply label each drawing and then discuss with you, a peer tutor, or an aide why the artifact is an example of that characteristic of civilization.

Advanced Learners

Offer a visual presentation assignment as an alternative to Processing 5. Have students use PowerPoint, poster board, or some other visual display to show that their community qualifies as a "civilization" based on the requirements listed in this chapter. Their presentations should include

- each of the seven characteristics discussed in the lesson.
- at least one example for each characteristic, labeled and represented with some kind of image (drawing, magazine cutout, computer graphic, and so forth).
- a sentence or two for each example, telling why this particular example fits the given characteristic.

Offer a one-page essay assignment as an alternative to Processing 5. Ask students to analyze the benefits to forming civilizations as opposed to the hunting-and-gathering bands that previously existed. In their essay, students should

- include an introductory paragraph that states their general position.
- choose three of the seven characteristics of civilization, and discuss how each characteristic would benefit a particular civilization.
- conclude with reference to today's civilizations and how those same three characteristics apply in today's societies.

Scientists sometimes describe a society or group of humans as "highly civilized." What do you think this means?

Fill in the empty spokes of the diagram below with words that describe characteristics of a society that is highly civilized. For each spoke, draw and label a simple example of that description. One spoke is completed for you.

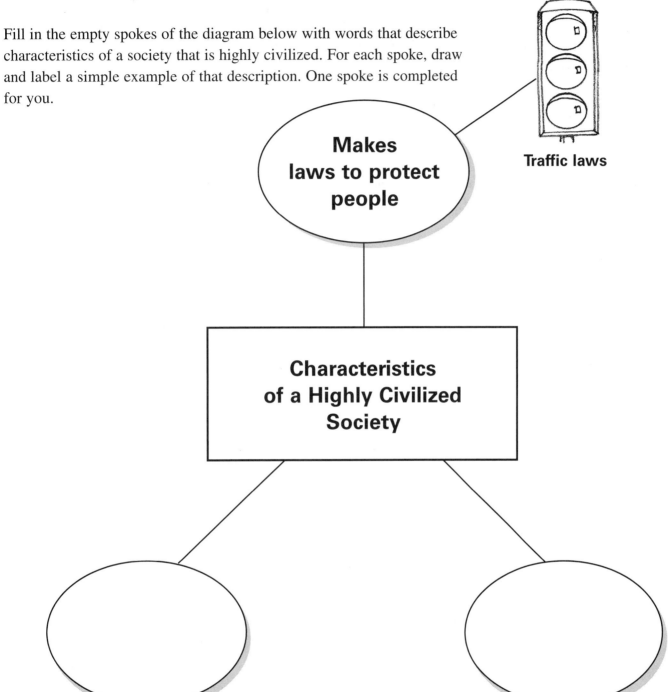

Makes laws to protect people

Traffic laws

Characteristics of a Highly Civilized Society

After reading one section of Chapter 5 in *History Alive! The Ancient World* and analyzing all the artifacts from ancient Sumer, follow these steps:

1. Find the oval in the diagrams on this and the following three pages that corresponds to the section you read.

2. In the space around that oval, make a simple drawing of *each artifact* you analyzed that you think is an example of that characteristic of civilization.

3. Next to each drawing, complete this sentence: *(Name of artifact) relates to this characteristic of civilization because...*

4. Complete the spoke diagram by connecting each drawing to the oval with a line.

**5.3
Stable Food
Supply**

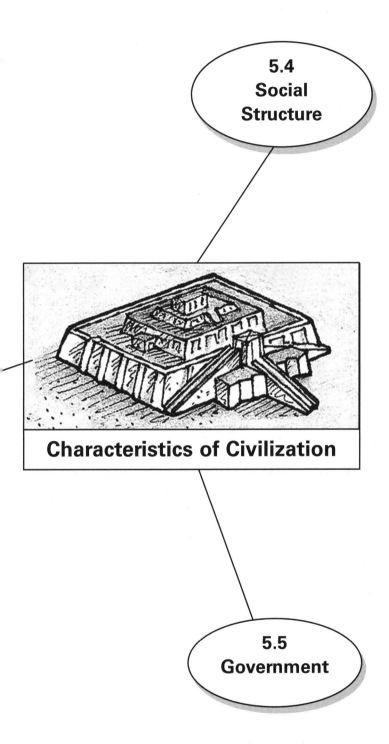

**5.4
Social
Structure**

Characteristics of Civilization

**5.5
Government**

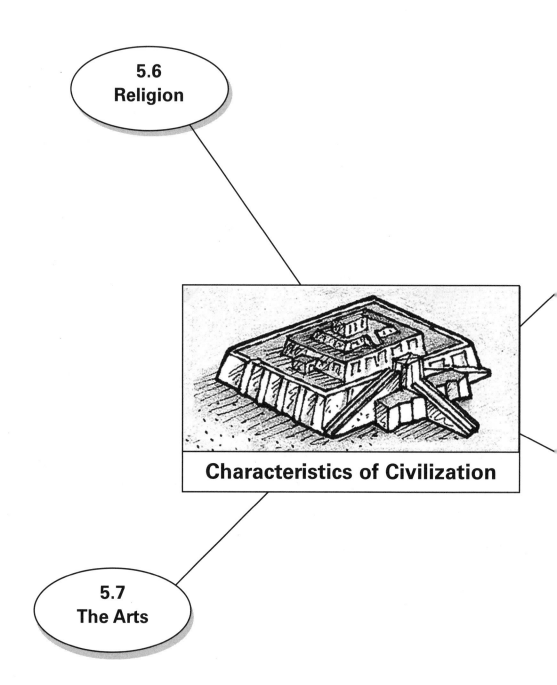

5.6
Religion

Characteristics of Civilization

5.7
The Arts

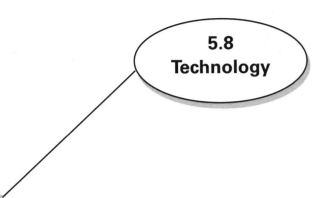

5.8 Technology

5.9 Writing

Complete the spoke diagram below by drawing or finding pictures of modern items that are examples of each characteristic of civilization. For each picture, follow these steps:

1. Glue or draw the picture next to the characteristic to which you think it is related.

2. Complete this sentence: *(Name of artifact) relates to this characteristic of civilization because….*

3. Draw a line connecting the picture to the oval.

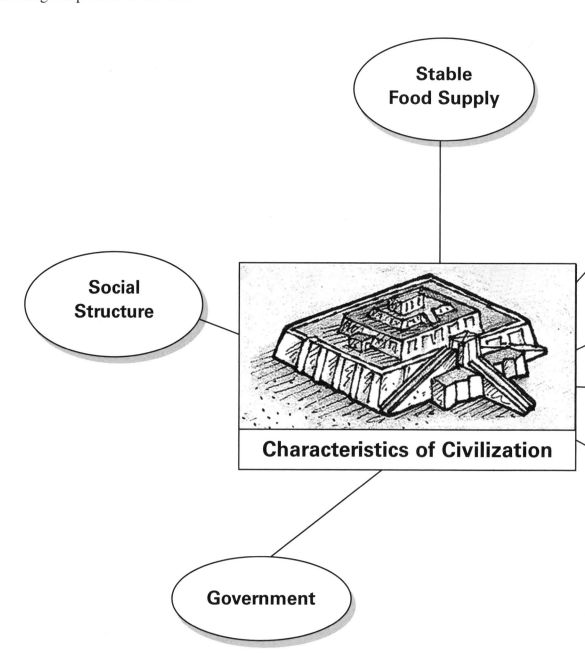

Stable Food Supply

Social Structure

Characteristics of Civilization

Government

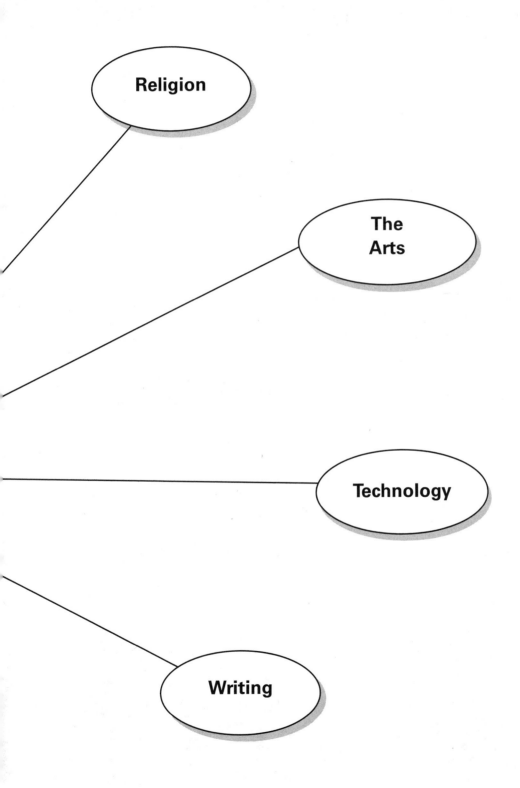

Religion

The Arts

Technology

Writing

CHAPTER 5

Panels from the Standard of Ur depict scenes of war and peace in ancient Sumer.

Was Ancient Sumer a Civilization?

5.1 Introduction

In the last chapter, you read about the rise of Sumerian city-states. In this chapter, you'll take a closer look at Sumerian **culture**. Like an archeologist, you'll consider evidence to try to answer a question about the distant past. The question is this: Was Sumer a **civilization**?

Until about 150 years ago, archeologists had no idea that the Sumerian people had lived at all. Then, in the mid 1800s, archeologists began finding artifacts in the area we call Mesopotamia. They dug up tablets, pottery, and the ruins of cities. They were surprised to find writing in a language they had never seen before.

By studying artifacts, archeologists have learned a lot about Sumer. One artifact is called the Standard of Ur. It was found where the ancient city of Ur once stood. You can see the standard on the opposite page. It is made of wood and decorated with pieces of shell and lapis lazuli, a semi-precious blue stone. It shows Sumerians in times of peace and war. Artifacts like this one can tell us a great deal about daily life in ancient Sumer.

We now know that the Sumerians had a complex society. Some of the things they invented, like the plow and writing, are still in use today. But can we call Sumer a civilization? Let's consider the evidence.

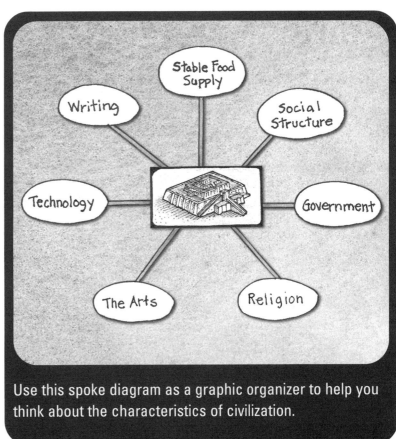

Use this spoke diagram as a graphic organizer to help you think about the characteristics of civilization.

5.2 Characteristic of Civilization

As you learned in the last chapter, Sumer was a challenging place to live. It had hot summers, little rain, and rivers that flooded the plains. Yet the Sumerians overcame these challenges. They built complex irrigation systems and large cities. By 3000 B.C.E., most Sumerians lived in powerful city-states like Ur, Lagash, and Uruk. But can we say that the Sumerians had created a civilization?

To answer this question, we need to think about what *civilization* means. What characteristics make a culture a civilization? Historians name several such characteristics, including these:

- a *stable food supply,* so that the people of a society have the food they need to survive
- a **social structure** with different social levels and jobs
- a *system of government,* so that life in the society is orderly
- a *religious system,* which involves a set of beliefs and forms of worship
- a *highly developed culture* that includes arts such as painting, architecture, music, and literature
- *advances in* **technology**
- a highly developed written *language*

Did Sumer have these characteristics? Let's find out what the evidence can tell us.

social structure the way a civilization is organized

technology the use of tools and other inventions for practical purposes

These two artifacts—one modern and one ancient Sumerian—are both examples of one characteristic of civilization. Can you name the characteristic?

5.3 Stable Food Supply

Civilizations need a stable food supply. A complex society can thrive only if its members have the food they need to survive.

Sumerians invented two things to help them create a stable food supply. You already know about one of these inventions—their complex irrigation systems. The Sumerians built networks of canals, dams, and reservoirs to provide their crops with a regular supply of water.

Their second invention was the plow. A plow is a tool for tilling (turning) the soil to prepare it for planting. Before the plow was invented, farmers used animal horns or pointed sticks to poke holes in the earth. Then they would plant seeds in the holes. This was a very slow way to farm. Farmers needed a faster way to prepare the land for planting.

The Sumerians made the first plow out of wood. One end was bent for cutting into the ground to turn the soil. Farmers pushed and pulled the plow along the ground themselves, or they used animals such as oxen to pull it.

Sumerians invented the plow. Today, families in Iraq (ancient Sumer) still farm the land using ox-drawn plows.

This man and child are standing in the ruins of the ancient city of Uruk.

5.4 Social Structure

Civilizations have a complex organization, or social structure. A social structure includes different jobs and social levels. People at higher levels have greater **status** than others.

Archeologists have found evidence that several classes of people lived in Sumer. At the top was an upper class, which included priests, land owners, and government officials. These people had the largest and most luxurious homes, near the center of the city. Their houses were two stories high. Evidence suggests they had whitewashed mud walls.

In the middle was the common class. This included merchants and craftspeople. The craftspeople included highly skilled metal-workers. They worked with such metals as gold, silver, tin, lead, copper, and bronze. With these materials, they made swords and arrowheads for the army. They made tools like plows and hoes for farmers. They also made luxury items, such as mirrors and jewelry, for the upper class.

The common class also included farmers and fishermen. They lived in small, mud-brick houses at the edge of the city. Farmers often worked to build or repair the irrigation systems. In times of war, they were forced to serve in the army.

At the very bottom of the social structure were slaves. They lived in their owners' homes and had no property of their own.

5.5 Government

All civilizations have a system of government to direct people's behavior and make life orderly. Sumerian city-states were ruled by kings. The Sumerians believed that their kings were chosen by the gods to rule in their place. This belief made their kings very powerful. It also helped strengthen the social order, since Sumerians believed they must obey the will of the gods.

Sumerian kings enforced the laws and collected taxes. They built temples and made sure irrigation systems were maintained.

A king also led his city-state's army. All the city-states needed armies because they were constantly fighting over land boundaries and the use of water. Leading the army was one of the king's most important jobs.

A Sumerian army included both professional soldiers and temporary citizen-soldiers. Some were foot soldiers. Others drove **chariots,** wheeled vehicles pulled by horses.

Kings had officials under them to help them with their duties. Governors ruled over outlying towns. **Scribes** helped record laws. The Sumerians were the first people to develop a system of written laws.

One special group of officials patrolled the canals. They looked for damage and made sure farmers didn't take water illegally.

chariot a two-wheeled vehicle pulled by a horse
scribe a person who writes

A king looks out from his palace walls over the city-state he rules.

5.6 Religion

All civilizations have a religious system. A religious system includes a set of beliefs, usually in a god or gods, together with forms of worship.

In Sumer, religious beliefs influenced every part of daily life. Sumerians tried to please the gods in all things, from growing crops to settling disputes. Religion bound them together in a common way of life.

Sumerians expressed their religious beliefs by building temples and religious towers called **ziggurats**. It was the king's duty to build and maintain the ziggurats. The towers were made of mud bricks and located near temples. They were so large that they could be seen from 20 miles away. Some were as high as eight stories and as wide as 200 feet.

The Sumerians believed that the gods lived in the ziggurats, and they built special temples at the top for them. Outside the ziggurat, they attached a long staircase so the gods could climb down to Earth. Kings and priests stood inside the towers to ask for the gods' blessings.

Sumerian statues also expressed their religious beliefs. Many of these statues were detailed and lifelike. They showed people worshipping the gods, often with their eyes gazing upward. The Sumerians believed that the gods were pleased when people showed them devotion, or love and obedience.

Sumerians had many kinds of religious ceremonies. Often musicians played at these ceremonies. Some ceremonies may have involved human sacrifice, the ritual killing of a person as an offering to the gods.

ziggurat an ancient Mesopotamian temple tower

This is a reconstruction of the ziggurat that once rose over the ancient city of Ur.

© Teachers' Curriculum Institute

5.7 The Arts

All civilizations have a highly developed culture, including the arts. Arts include creative forms of expression such as painting, architecture, and music.

There were many kinds of artists and craftspeople in Sumer. Sumerian metalworkers made practical objects, like weapons and cups. They also made decorative items, such as mirrors and jewelry. Sumerian architects designed temples and ziggurats.

Music was another important art in Sumer. The Sumerians believed that music brought joy to the gods and people alike. Musicians played instruments and sang during temple ceremonies. They wrote love songs and entertained guests at feasts.

Musicians played many instruments, including drums and pipes. One favorite was a small harp called a *lyre*. Lyres were wooden instruments made of a sound box and strings. A wooden bar held the strings in place at the top. Lyre makers often decorated their instruments with precious stones and carvings made of horn. These decorations show how much the Sumerians valued music.

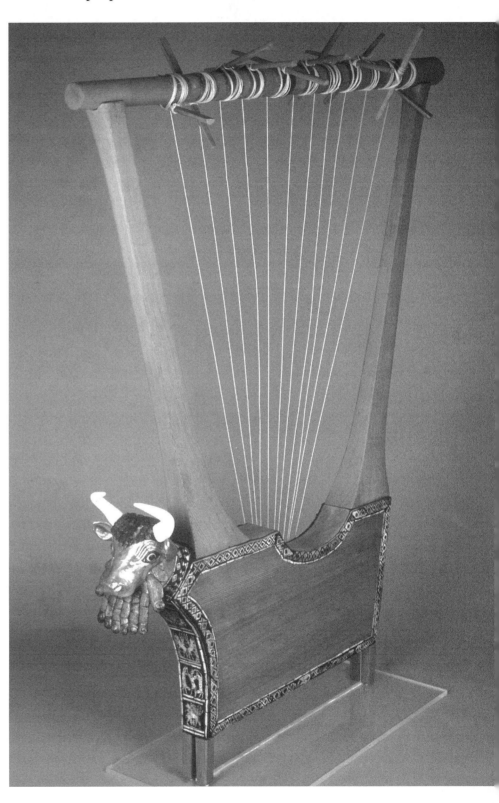

This fancy lyre has the head of a bull decorating its sound box. A musician would strum the strings to play musical notes.

5.8 Technology

All civilizations create new forms of technology, or practical tools and inventions. The Sumerians made several technological advances.

The Sumerians' most important invention was the wheel. The earliest examples of the wheel date back to 3500 B.C.E. Sumerian potters, or pottery makers, used wheels as a surface for shaping clay into pots. Potters' wheels spun, flat side up, on an axle. Sumerians discovered that a wheel that was flipped onto its edge could be rolled forward. They used this discovery to create wheeled carts for farmers and chariots for the army. They built the wheels by clamping pieces of wood together.

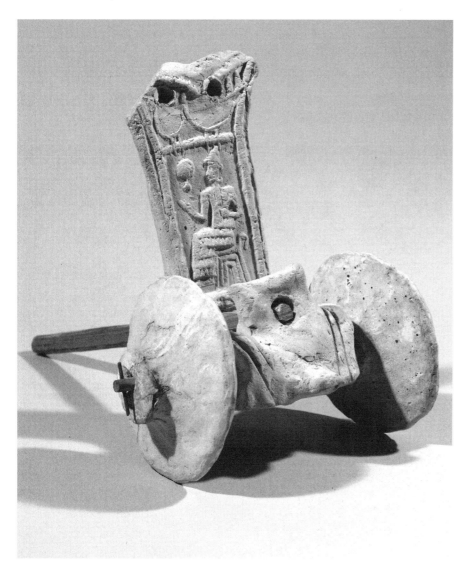

This model shows a wheeled chariot used in the Sumerian army. Chariots were pulled by a horse while a soldier stood behind the shield.

arch an upside-down U- or V-shaped structure that supports weight above it, as in a doorway

It would be hard to imagine a more powerful invention than the wheel. Before the wheel, people had to drag their goods on flat-bottomed carts called *sledges*. The sledges often got stuck in mud, and they couldn't support heavy loads. Wheeled carts made it much easier to move goods over long distances. Oxen could pull three times more weight on wheeled carts than they could on sledges.

Another technological advance was the **arch**. Sumerian arches were inverted (upside down) U- or V-shaped structures built above doorways. To build arches, the Sumerians stacked bricks made of clay and straw so that they rose in steps from the walls until they met in the center.

Arches added strength and beauty to Sumerian buildings. They became a common feature of temple entrances and upper-class homes. Some historians say the arch is the Sumerians' greatest architectural achievement.

5.9 Writing

A final characteristic of civilizations is a highly developed written language. The Sumerians created a written language called **cuneiform**. This name comes from the Latin word for "wedge." The Sumerians used a wedge-shaped stylus (a sharp, pointed tool) to etch their writing in clay tablets.

Sumerians developed cuneiform around 2400 B.C.E. The earliest examples of cuneiform show that it was used to record information about the goods Sumerians exchanged with one another. At first, they may have used as many as 2,000 symbols to stand for ideas and sounds. Over time, they were able to reduce this number to about 700.

Cuneiform was based on an earlier, simpler form of writing that used pictographs. **Pictographs** are symbols that stand for real objects, such as a snake or water. Scribes drew the symbols with a sharpened reed on wet clay. When the clay dried, the marks became a permanent record.

This relief sculpture shows scribes using a clay tablet and stylus.

5.10 Chapter Summary

Was Sumerian culture a civilization? It had all the characteristics you read about at the start of this chapter. The people of Sumer created a stable food supply. Their society had a complex social structure. They had a system of government, headed by kings. They had a religious system with priests, temples, and ziggurats. They had highly developed arts, technologies, and written language. For these reasons, historians call Sumer one of the world's first civilizations.

Sumerian civilization lasted about 1,500 years, from 3500 to 2000 B.C.E. What happened to the Sumerians? What new cultures developed in Mesopotamia? In the next chapter, you'll find out.

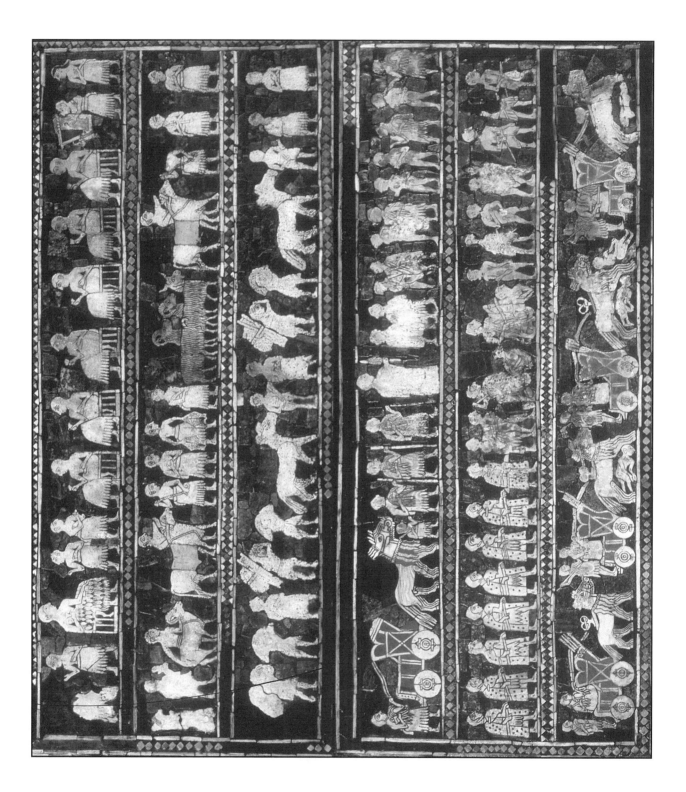

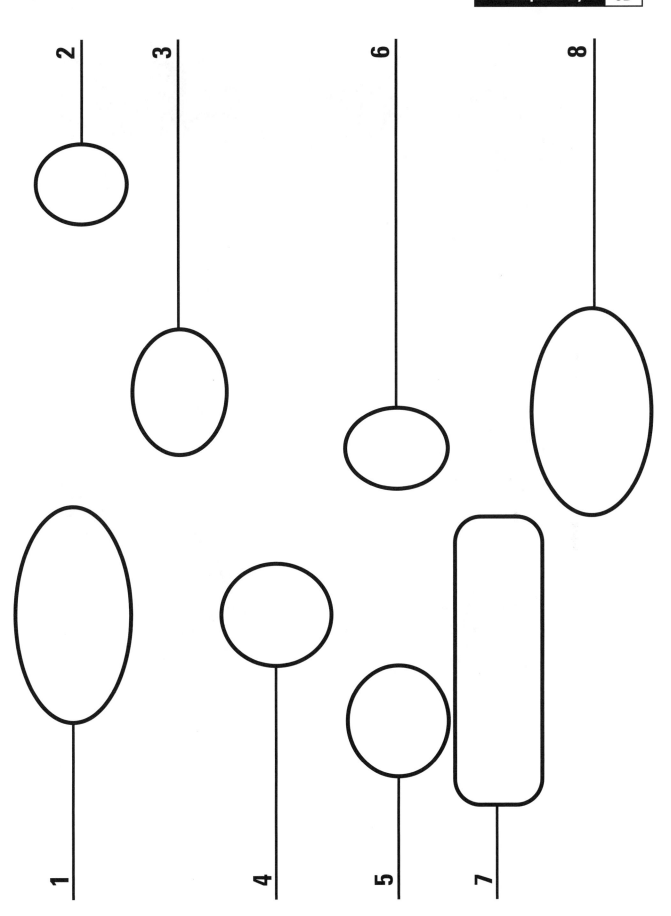

Archeologist's notes: On this clay tablet, scribes from the Temple of Bau recorded the amount of barley (a grain) that each of the workers and their families will receive.

Archeologist's notes: This small statue of a married couple was found in the rubble of a religious shrine. The original statue had eyes made of shells and semiprecious stones. It was probably left at the shrine as a gift to the gods.

Archeologist's notes: This impression was made from a stone seal. It shows two gods. One god has a hand in the shape of a scorpion. The other is using a plow.

Archeologist's notes: This clay seal shows King Ur-Nammu (seated) appointing Hashhamer as one of his governors. The cuneiform inscription on the seal says, "Ur-Nammu, the mighty hero, king of Ur; Hashhamer, the governor of Ishkun-Sin, his servant."

This carved stone seal was rolled across a slab of clay to create the scene shown above.

Archeologist's notes: This small copper statue shows a Sumerian chariot being pulled by four donkeys. This kind of chariot was probably used by Sumerian soldiers.

Archeologist's notes: This gold cup was created by Sumerian artisans, probably to be used at banquets. These banquets were generally for the members of the upper classes of Sumerian society.

Archeologist's notes: This bronze statue shows King Ur-Nammu carrying a basket of bricks on his head. This probably represents the fact that one of the king's main responsibilities was to build and maintain the temples, even though he didn't actually do the work himself. The inscription around the body of the statue records the restoration of the temple of Inana, the patron god of Uruk.

Archeologist's notes: This lyre—a stringed musical instrument—was decorated with gold and semiprecious stones. It was found in the tomb of a Sumerian queen. Royal musicians may have played this instrument to entertain the queen and her court. The music you hear is similar to the kind of music the queen might have listened to.

Credits

p. 8: Etosha National Park, Namibia; Jeremy Woodhouse/Getty Images/PhotoDisc. **p. 9:** Pyramid at Giza, sphinx in front; Neil Beer/Getty Images/PhotoDisc. **p. 10:** Amber Fort near Jaipur, India; Glen Allison/Getty Images/PhotoDisc. **p. 11:** Great Wall of China; Tim Hall/Getty Images/PhotoDisc. **p. 12:** View of the Parthenon and Acropolis, Athens, Greece; Scala/Art Resource, NY. **p. 13:** Colosseum, Rome, Italy; Sami Sarkis/Getty Images/PhotoDisc. **p. 20:** Greenstone seal of Hashhamer and impression: Third Dynasty of Ur, ca. 2100 B.C.E.; ©Trustees of the British Museum, London. **p. 27:** Doug Roy. **p. 28:** Doug Roy. **p. 33:** Doug Roy. **p. 35:** Doug Roy. **p. 36:** Doug Roy. **p. 38:** Doug Roy. **p. 40:** Both sides of the Standard of Ur (detail), illustration of scenes of war and peace; worked in shell, red limestone, and lapis lazuli, bitumen inlay; ©Trustees of the British Museum, London. **p. 41:** Doug Roy. **p. 42, left:** Reverse of U.S. penny; Teachers' Curriculum Institute. **p. 42, right:** Phoenician galley ship on a coin of Sidon, Mesopotamian period, ca. 4th C. B.C.E.; British Museum, London; © Winfield Parks/National Geographic Image Collection. **p. 43:** Boy plowing with buffalo in Azerbaijan area of Iran; © Roger Wood/Corbis. **p. 44:** Sumerian ruins of Uruk; © Nik Wheeler/Corbis. **p. 45:** Nebuchadrezzar II, Chaldean king of Babylon; North Wind Picture Archives. **p. 46:** Ziggurat of Ur, Iraq, Sumerian city ca. 4500–400 B.C.E.; Robert Harding. **p. 47:** Reconstruction of a lyre found in the grave of Queen Pu-abi, Royal Cemetery, Ur, Iraq; ©Trustees of the British Museum, London. **p. 48:** Baked clay model of a chariot, 17 x 15 cm; period of the Amorite dynasties, 2000–1595 B.C.E.; © Erich Lessing/Art Resource, NY. **p. 49:** Relief of scribes using tablet and stylus; ©Trustees of the British Museum, London. **p. 50 (Transparency 5A):** Both sides of the Standard of Ur; ©Trustees of the British Museum, London. **p. 52 (Placard 5A):** A Sumerian clay tablet with incised cuneiform characters tallying sheep and goats, from Tello, ancient Mesopotamia; © Gianni Dagli Orti/Corbis. **p. 53 (Placard 5B):** Man and woman embracing, statue from Nippur, early dynastic period, 2600 B.C.E.; Iraq Museum, Baghdad, Iraq; © Scala/Art Resource, NY. **p. 54 (Placard 5C):** Sumerian cylinder seal impression showing two gods and a plow; Tell Asmar, Esnunna, Ashnunaq; ©The Oriental Institute Museum of the University of Chicago. **p. 55 (Placard 5D):** Greenstone seal of Hashhamer and impression: Third Dynasty of Ur, ca. 2100 B.C.E.; ©Trustees of the British Museum, London. **p. 56 (Placard 5E):** Bronze chariot from Tell Agrab; early dynastic (Sumerian), 2600 B.C.E.; height 2¾"; Iraq Museum, Baghdad, Iraq; © Scala/Art Resource, NY. **p. 57 (Placard 5):** Queen Pu-abi feeding cup, Sumer, 2000 B.C.E.; © Boltin Picture Library. **p. 58 (Placard 5G):** Bronze statue of King Ur-Nammur of Nippur, Sumerian, ca 2100 B.C.E.; Iraq Museum, Baghdad, Iraq; © Scala/Art Resource, NY. **p. 59 (Placard 5H):** Ur bull lyre, Sumer, 3500–2000 B.C.E.; © Boltin Picture Library.

DATE DUE